Wide Awake

Maya Elmouhawesse

BookLeaf Publishing

Presentation by *BookLeaf Publishing*

Web: www.bookleafpub.com

E-mail: info@bookleafpub.com

ISBN: 9789357748834

First edition 2023

Overall, I dedicate "Wide Awake" simply to myself. It has been a self love letter to myself that heightened the realization that I am of value, I have a talent, and I have a future. Simply put, I created this for and by myself. For me.

ACKNOWLEDGEMENT

I was fortunate to have the chance to enroll in a creative writing course during my junior year of high school. I had a lot of trouble with the short stories we wrote in the beginning. The amount of information to include and the unique writing methods utilized to keep readers interested. Well, I had trouble with that. Then, we got to the poetry portion, and something inside of me ignited that hadn't previously. I previously believed that I would be terrible. I didn't know what a stanza was, if poetry had to rhyme, or how to construct my sentences. Nonetheless, there were countless opportunities, and I was informed that my poetry was important. I began with that creative writing course and ended with a continuation of poetry. There were so many opportunities I was supported for, and my teacher strongly advised me to submit these poems to places, and my dad urged me to post them on my website. I thank both of you for seeing me when I couldn't.

Recess!

As kids we play with anyone and everyone
Unaware of the judgements
Innocent to what makes someone a character
Purely running in a game of tag
Legs going up and down on the swings
Humidity flying through our hair
Two dimples high in the air
Playtime feels like forever
Every minute is spent worthwhile
Four legs on the monkey bars
Upside down hanging from our feet
Anyone is allowed to play
Until playtime is over
Back to reality

Pigtails

My favorite hairstyle was pigtails
My mommy used to do my pigtails
My daddy also did my pigtails
My peers used to pull on my pigtails
My hair was once hung on a hook by my pigtails
My candy was stuck in my pigtails
My inner child comes out with pigtails
My head turns side to side with pigtails

Hot Summer's Day

S'mores cooking by the campfire
The smell of coal and smoke

Ice cream truck is on its way
The sound of music appeals to ears

People soon belong on the sidewalks
Walking their dogs and on their bicycles

Spontaneous amusement trips
Handprints lasting under the sun

Drawings of vibrancy along the driveway
Children tend to their expression

Season of illuminations in the sky
Celebration of our independence day

Halloween Night

Drops from the sink
Shattered glass from the floor
A shadow in the closet
Cuts on your hands
Friday the 13th plays
Individual through the window
Candy searched for substance
Gas stove magically turned on
Floor creaks from around the corner
Autumn falls leaves drop from gloom
Saws being behind the run
A mysterious night it can be.

Education System

Wanna go to the bathroom?
Raise your hand
Get a pass
Write a note

Need to stay home?
Call in sick
Get a doctor's note
Make up your work

Help with homework?
Look at the notes
Teach it to yourself
Cry and ask for help

Have to pass this test?
Determines your intelligence
70% of your grade is lowered
Maybe take a peek next time

Need a second to breathe?
Skip class
Get a detention
Go to the counselor's office

Wanna do any school event?
Attend useless clubs
Pay a ton of money for dances
Stay unrecognized beneath popular kids

Why do we wake up so early?
Why are we punished for feeling emotions?
Why don't we get to choose to pursue our
passions full-time?
Why do we sit for hours doing nothing?
Why do we receive an A+ for just writing our
name?

My Name Is

Simple, simple names
Like Olivia,
Sophia,
Emma,
Madison,
Elizabeth

Attendance
"Is May-uh Elmo-how weese here?"
Job Interview
"I hope I don't butcher your name… Mia
Elmoo-ha-wise"
Graduation
"Next up is Miyah Elmu-hay-wesi"

Let's clear the air
I have a culture within me
This is my identity
It's Maya
And my last name is Elmouhawesse
My name is Maya Elmouhawesse

The DMV

It's a free booklet, just need to pick it up
Skim through it, simple
Told, "it's common sense"
Dad picked me up from a sleepover
Everyone told me it is the easiest thing ever
Walking in there you can hear people breath and
swallow
Went in with too much confidence
I failed.

Made it a plan to study with my friend
Both of us failed before, I didn't feel alone
Spent the second day together swapping turns
Succeeded on every online test
Met at the DMV together the next day
Fingers crossed to pass together
She passed
I failed.

Third time's the charm they say
Took almost a year to pick up the book again
Only person in the family who isn't smart
Who didn't pass the first time
I went in there with no interest, completely
winged it

My dad had the resilience and a plan to try again
So, as you can tell
I failed.

Four days later, Saturday
Gloomy, distant, and only wanting to be alone
No excuse not to try again
Hadn't studied or reviewed all week
No confidence, no feeling prepared
Walked in completely intimidated
But, was seated next to the most precious girl
I wasn't alone this time
We checked on one another
Next thing I know, she ran out eagerly with a
smile
Then, two minutes later, I walked out with my
piece of paper
I passed

My time at the DMV was done
Until, I come back to try for my actual driver's
license

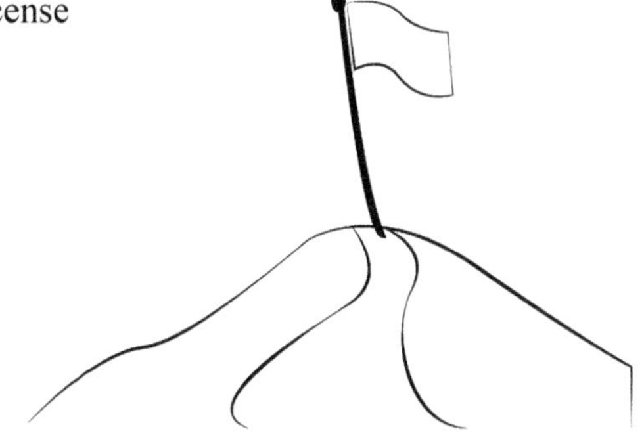

Stages of Change

Curious about how it differs
Excited for a new world
Guilty of what is left behind
Anxious to be in a new environment
Insecure because you feel so behind
Tired towards adjustments
Wishful for your old life back
Motivated to fit in
Driven about catching up
Hopeless because you feel unrecognized
Resilient to keep going in efforts
Confused why you can't find comfort
Disappointed because it's not what you thought
Shameful that you don't find positives
Ambitious to create new goals
Depressed at times you feel defeated
Peaceful that it was the right decision in the end

Angel's Hands

Olive skin fingers
Pink perfected nails
Water dumped through your hair
With her hand on your head
Running her nails as she blow drys
Lotioned Aveeno body
Memorable back scratches
Began from your back to your arm

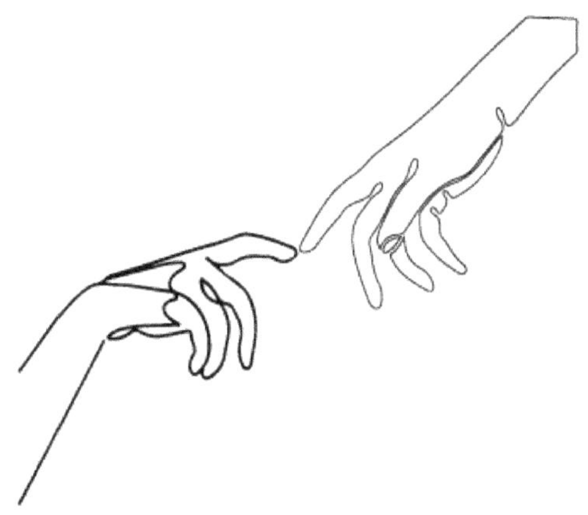

i finally did it

5 psychiatrists
4 antidepressants
3 therapists
2 mental wards
1 life

No hesitation, numb expression
Home all evening, same spot
Make sure to smile at dad
Pretend to pack lunch
But really packing pills

10 citaloprams
9 prozacs
8 ibuprofens
7 effexors
6 zolofts

Grab a full glass of water
Lay in bed comfortably
Pick up 2 handfuls
Swallow without thought
It's finally the end, it's done.

four-sided box

A four-sided box
No light
No color
No comfort
No freedom
No control
No hygiene
No family
No voice
No outside
No home
A four-sided box

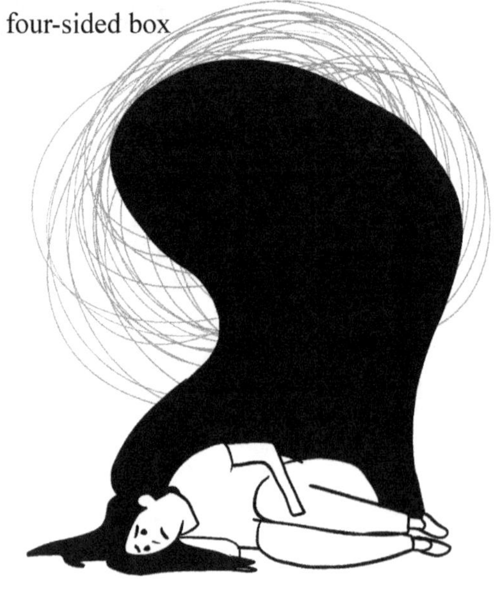

Take a Guess?

It's considered a holiday to some
Occurs once a year
Parties are usually thrown
Slowly gets higher

Not sure?

A bittersweet celebration of age
Lifeless day of rebirth
Stacks kept of useless cards
Tomato cheeks bursting

Have an idea yet?

All to some to none sticks blown
Googly eyes surrounded
Anxiety of incorrect expression
Worry for everyone's satisfactory

Wanna take a guess now?

"nothing has changed"

Past, present, and future
Time machine, currency, or psychic abilities
The time you are born and the time you die
All significant moments in time

Blindly following a rewarded leader
Stone weapons to metal ones
Smart weapons and nuclear bombs

Johnson and Trump impeached
Bubonic plague and COVID-19
Vietnam and Ukraine
Princess Diana and Michelle Obama

Romeo & Juliet to Tony & Maria
Slavery now known as BLM
Rest cure delusion is medicated and real
History speaks for itself

Relief

That feeling of closing the last tab
That feeling of checking off every task
That feeling of throwing away all those now
unneeded papers
That feeling of cleaning the last dish
That feeling of finishing the last episode of a
season
That feeling of completing the last piece to the
puzzle
That feeling of sleeping knowing there won't be
interruptions
That feeling of folding the last piece of laundry
That feeling of ending on the last page of a book
That feeling of finally getting that piece of food
out of your teeth
That feeling of dumping the supplies from your
book bag out

What do these all have in common? It's a relief.

No Shame

Face is too dry
Face is too oily
Eyebrows are over-plucked
Eyebrows are bushy
Nose is like Pinocchio
Nose is like Voldemort's
Lips should be injected
Lips should be natural
Skin is ghostly
Skin is blackface
Body is hourglass shape
Body is anorexic
Teeth are bucked
Teeth are crooked
Facial hair is hideous
Facial hair is attractive
Hands are elderly
Hands are soft
Ribcage is wide
Ribcage is nonexistent

Male

I spend my days in silence
Glares and comments to my sides
Popular girls and popular men
They criticize everything
Gym class they stare at your ass
Or make fun of the fat on your body jiggle as
you run
Laugh how you complain to throw a ball
You answer a question and they call you a know
it all
They say you're vulgar and too chill
When it's them overreacting like a toddler
Because it was just a "joke"
But how long do these "jokes" last?
Splashes of water being thrown on me
The discomfort
Offensive tone that makes me run to my seat
Male teachers agreeing with their boys
A dominance like no other
Makes us fearful and attacked
Males are no friend of mine

Sisters

You are older
I am younger
You are pale
I am tan
You are taller
I am shorter
You have straight hair
I have curly hair
You like books
I like movies
You are the moon
I am the sun
You are an introvert
I am an extrovert
You need order
I need chaos
You don't see flaws
I only see wrongs

GIRLY GIRL

She calmly turns to her left shoulder
Gently, shuts off her pink alarm
Gracefully, attends to her skin regimen
Wearing a juicy couture pink, silk robe
Just to move luscious hair behind her ears

With every drop of facial oil landing in perfect
time
She presses it into the glistening skin
At ease, comes natural beauty
Yet, it's covered so diligently with darker-shaded
foundation
And no longer that skin is present

Small, black sets of detail to her eyes
Not done yet because the hair comes next
Such beautiful curly hair just to get damaged
A 400-degree straightener drowns out the wave
She's almost ready to go for the day

Up next we have the OOTD
Not too short to be dress coded, or long enough
to not see
She gradually ignores the weathers behalf
Wear what makes you look happy and wealthy
The beauty is disrupted because it's not how you
feel

Routine

Phone goes off
Flip on your stomach and left arm hanging
5 am workout while watching football
Quick shower, suit and tie
Kiss wife goodnight
Energy drinks to go and coffee breath to start
Accounting until 6 pm
Clients complaining until you're deaf
Bonus arrives in the mail
Large footsteps appear at the door
3 children hug and jump with joy
Wife kisses you
Dinner is on the table ready
Daddy's home
This is where he ends up everyday

The Unreal

Imagine candy land coming to life
Or a fiesta everyday celebrating not being alive
Will it be dark and gloomy?
Pink fluffy clouds and sunshine?
Do unicorns live there?
Or mermaids? Bigfoot?
Is it made up of our fantasies and dreams
A button that makes any dish you want become
real
Giant sundaes like in shark boy and lava girl
Perfect bodies naked and free
Rollercoasters with no waiting lines
Food falling from the sky
No wars, no crimes
Do we get to look down and see who misses us?
I can't tell if that is selfish or simply evil

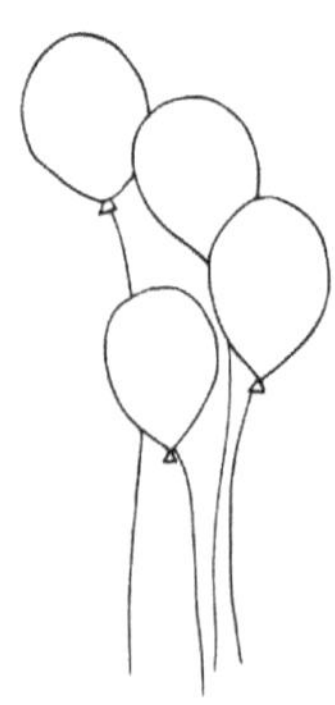

Chaos

Life constantly needs to be on the go
Errands always continue to grow
Too impatient for things to go slow
Have two jobs at all times to make enough doe

The loudness helps drown out all my thoughts
Translations often come off as whatnots
Yet I'm the one who often calls people a snot
Which is funny because I struggle with lots

It's easy to keep going when I'm occupied
Honestly, I don't know how I get things when
I'm barely qualified
At this point, to slow it down, there should be a
homicide
If that person is me then this is now
hypothesized